PIANO • VOCAL • GUITAR

ISBN 0-634-07675-2

HAL•LEONARD®
CORPORATION

7777 W. BLUEMOUND RD. P.O. BOX 13819 MILWAUKEE, WI 53213

Visit Hal Leonard Online at
www.halleonard.com

RIGHT WHERE I BELONG

Words and Music by BRAD ARNOLD,
ROBERT HARRELL, CHRISTOPHER HENDERSON
and MATTHEW ROBERTS

too man-y peo-ple and too man-y things, and it makes me feel like hell.
I get dis-tract-ed and car-ried a-way, and it's been this way too long.

And you're half gone as I can see, and
Well, I don't know what you need from me 'cause

all of this she says to me.
all I know is what I can see.

There's too man-y ques-tions and too

man-y strings and they won't keep their-self tied. On a roll-

4

IT'S NOT ME

Words and Music by BRAD ARNOLD,
ROBERT HARRELL, CHRISTOPHER HENDERSON
and MATTHEW ROBERTS

Moderately slow Rock

Nev - er mind the face ___ that you put on ___ in front of ___ me ___
For - get a - bout this trip ___ that you've been on, ___ or so it ___ seems, ___

LET ME GO

Words and Music by BRAD ARNOLD,
ROBERT HARRELL, CHRISTOPHER HENDERSON
and MATTHEW ROBERTS

Moderate Rock

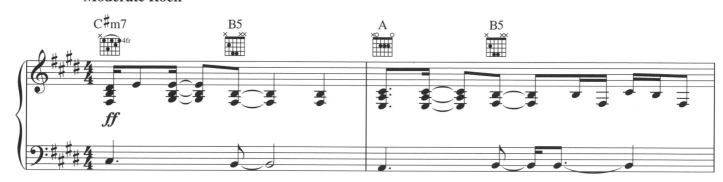

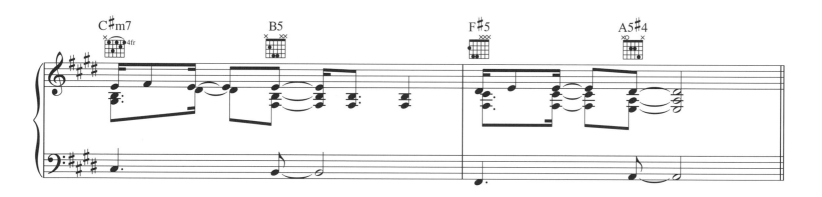

One __ more kiss __ could be __ the best __ thing.
I dream a - head __ to what __ I hope __ for.

BE SOMEBODY

Words and Music by BRAD ARNOLD,
ROBERT HARRELL, CHRISTOPHER HENDERSON
and MATTHEW ROBERTS

LANDING IN LONDON

Words and Music by BRAD ARNOLD,
ROBERT HARRELL, CHRISTOPHER HENDERSON
and MATTHEW ROBERTS

Slowly, with feeling

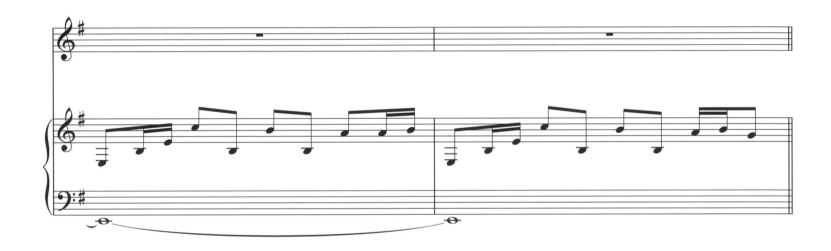

I woke up to-day __ in Lon - don

Whoa, _____ whoa. _____

And all these days _____ I spend _____ a -

CODA

D

'cause all I think ___ a - bout ___ is you. _____

mp

Em

poco rit.

THE REAL LIFE

Words and Music by BRAD ARNOLD,
ROBERT HARRELL, CHRISTOPHER HENDERSON
and MATTHEW ROBERTS

That's___ where I'll___ find out.___

D.S.S. al Coda II

CODA II

bet - ter part ___ of ___ me. ___

sub. *mp*

BEHIND THOSE EYES

Words and Music by BRAD ARNOLD,
ROBERT HARRELL, CHRISTOPHER HENDERSON
and MATTHEW ROBERTS

Moderate Rock

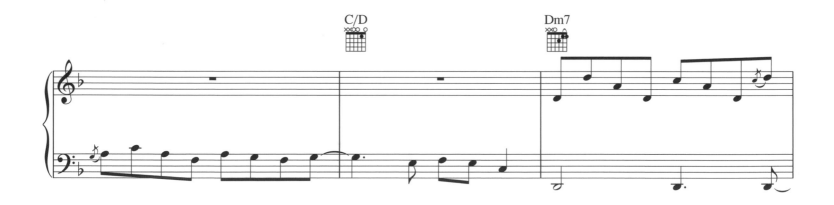

NEVER WILL I BREAK

Words and Music by BRAD ARNOLD,
ROBERT HARRELL, CHRISTOPHER HENDERSON
and MATTHEW ROBERTS

Slow Rock

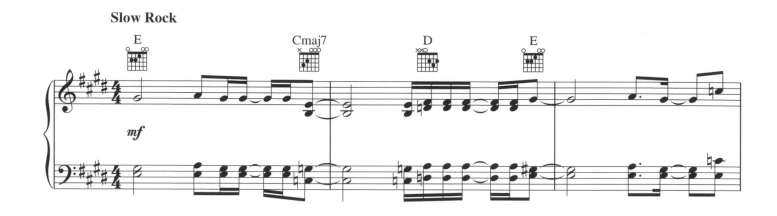

FATHER'S SONS

Words and Music by BRAD ARNOLD,
ROBERT HARRELL, CHRISTOPHER HENDERSON
and MATTHEW ROBERTS

Slow Rock

In the glare of a ne-on sign, ___ she laid her bod-y ___ down. ___ The

LIVE FOR TODAY

Words and Music by BRAD ARNOLD,
ROBERT HARRELL, CHRISTOPHER HENDERSON
and MATTHEW ROBERTS

MY WORLD - BIGGER THAN ME

Words and Music by BRAD ARNOLD,
ROBERT HARRELL, CHRISTOPHER HENDERSON
and MATTHEW ROBERTS

HERE BY ME

Words and Music by BRAD ARNOLD,
ROBERT HARRELL, CHRISTOPHER HENDERSON
and MATTHEW ROBERTS

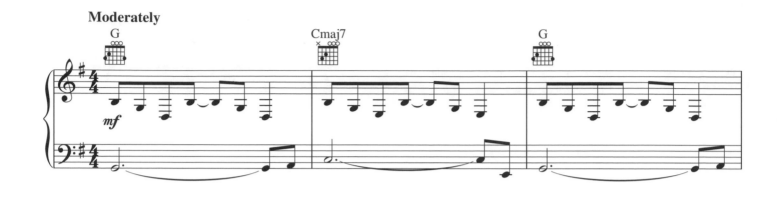

I hope you're do - ing fine ___ out ___ there ___ with - out ___
I can't take ___ an - oth - er ___ day ___ with - out ___

___ me ___ 'cause I'm not do - ing so ___
___ you ___ 'cause, ba - by, I could nev - er make ___